DRIVE-TIME MEDITATIONS

DRIVE-TIME
MEDITATIONS

Find Purpose on Your Commute

Donna Apidone

LUMINARE PRESS
WWW.LUMINAREPRESS.COM

DRIVE-TIME MEDITATIONS
Find Purpose on Your Commute
Copyright © 2022 by Donna Apidone

Printed in the United States of America

Cover Photo by César Couto on Unsplash
Author Photo by Raymond Formanek

Luminare Press
442 Charnelton St.
Eugene, OR 97401
www.luminarepress.com

LCCN: 2022911127
ISBN: 979-8-88679-030-6

In memory of my parents.
One taught metaphysics. One did not.
The balance of life.

INTRODUCTION

With change comes adaptation. We are not always in charge of change, but we can take responsibility for how we adapt. The few moments we find to process our thoughts – in the car, on the train, even in the shower – may be our only opportunities to set the tone for the day or evening.

Your morning and afternoon commutes are key times for reflection. They are the times when you have brilliant, creative ideas. They are times when you make decisions. The reason for clarity in the morning and afternoon is that you are receptive. You can block out other voices and listen to your own inner voice.

This book will not teach you how to meditate. I am not that teacher. My job is to guide you to your Purpose. These pages connect you to something within. My words help you to eliminate distractions so you can focus on more meaningful pursuits.

A glance at any of these one-page meditations provides you with encouragement for the rest of the day. Each one sets a tone of calm. Words have power. These words offer strength and direction.

I've kept the meditations to a single page for a couple of reasons. First and foremost, I want you to stay alert on your commute. When I read or listen to long meditations, I fade into sleepiness. Even as I reflect on matters of mindfulness, it's easy to doze. These short pieces won't make you drowsy. They will inspire you to be engaged and alert.

The second reason for short meditations is that brevity is my natural communication style. In my career as a public radio host, I've learned to edit everything I say to less than a minute. As I interview people, their voices, not mine, are what the audience wants to hear. Each of these concise pages serves as a prompt. I suggest a topic for your reflection, and your voice creates a response.

I have been asked how I can listen to news coverage, as part of my work, for six hours a day without getting depressed. The answer is simple: Purpose. It is my job to look beyond my emotions so the audience can feel compassion for people in the news. When I stopped looking at myself and saw my place in the world, I found my Purpose. These meditations ask you to look beyond your needs to discover your greater role.

This book has an element of spirituality without mention of religion. I think of spirituality as the discovery of and connection to something bigger than myself. My friends who do not consider themselves spiritual still believe in something. Some say nature sustains them. Some count on poetry. Scientists understand that they have not yet found all the answers. Musicians take yet a different path.

My goal is to provide direction without dogma. Feel free to fill in your own connection as you consider the essence of the message.

I am here to guide you to your unique Purpose. You are here to embrace it. When I speak to groups and lead classes, I see looks of delight and relief as participants find their place in the world. You will find, as they have, that your Purpose will emerge. These meditations allow you to move beyond change to adaptation.

For just a moment, I close my eyes.
I listen.
The sound around me is clear.
I hear a pattern ... a rhythm ... a beat.
It repeats.
Gentle, soft, ongoing.
I welcome this sound of external
Becoming internal.
I listen.
The rhythm of sound continues.
I compare it to the sound of my heartbeat.
My pulse,
The rhythmic pattern of my life,
A sound that goes unnoticed.
I hear it now, so soft it is barely audible.
In my ears, a gentle heartbeat.
In my wrists and my fingertips, in my ankles and toes,
I hear, I feel, my heartbeat.
I focus on the rhythm.
I notice its continuity, its consistency.
This gentle sound is uniquely mine.
I settle within, comforted by every beat,
By the spaces between the beats.
I breathe.
I listen.

When I connect, I know what to do.

When I have empathy,

I know my Purpose.

When I put myself in the place of others,

When I have compassion,

I cannot walk away.

I have to stop,

Determine what I can do,

And do it.

By taking small steps,

One person can change the world.

I am that person.

I am the person whose actions reverberate.

I am the person who cares enough

To feed.

To listen.

To encourage a new law.

If I can change the direction of one life,

I have lived my Purpose.

The world is counting on me.

When I have empathy,

I know my Purpose.

When I connect,

I know what to do.

Peace is
The quiet place
In between extremes.
Peace is the middle ground.
As you become centered,
You feel peace.
Peace falls into your center.
It is a release from the day,
From the week.
A release from everything.
Peace is free of decisions.
Peace is free of charge.
Peace is freedom.
Peace is easy to find.
Peace is within you.
Peace be with you.
Peace be still.

I sit in this vehicle, and I prepare for the next movement of my journey.

I take this moment to be calm.

I keep my eyes open. I stay aware of my surroundings.

I allow myself to be sheltered in a protective bubble.

I am safe. I feel and hear my breath.

As I attend to what is happening around me,

I notice the calm inside.

I inhale, a long, slow, easy breath.

My exhale is even longer, allowing all air to leave my body before I inhale again.

From within my protective bubble, I see people around me.

I recognize them as fellow travelers.

We have different destinations, yet we are on the same journey.

This travel, this traffic, this meditation ... just a moment.

Time means nothing here. Destination is a figment.

I focus instead on the journey.

I focus on our shared experience.

As I focus, "I" becomes "we."

I share my calm breathing with all around me.

Humanity.

People around the world say they feel frustration.

We can work together to ease that feeling.

As you breathe,

Envision just one person.

Breathe in and see the light within that person.

Breathe out and release pain on behalf of that person.

As you continue to breathe, remember this:

Every being shines a light.

Like a candle, we can expand the brightness of the light.

Like a lamp, we can replace a dull light with greater voltage.

We each have the power to help another,

Even someone we don't know.

The first thing is to acknowledge their light.

Look around you. See the light in every being.

Everyone is a light in this world.

Give them what it takes to shine – a smile, a kind word.

Give them your heart, encouragement, love.

Breathe in and see the light in each person.

Breathe out and release their pain.

Be the light that shines.

I wait.

At first, there is boredom.

I sigh.

And then, a fascination begins to grow.

I notice the colors. I hear the sounds.

I wonder about them.

I wonder.

I see this opportunity to witness my surroundings.

I take this opportunity to look.

To see.

To acknowledge.

This moment will pass.

There will never be another moment like it.

Now it is over. The moment is gone.

I am changed.

I remain fascinated.

The light surrounds us.

The light is in us.

We see with our hearts.

We envision.

Everything around us is for our consideration.

For enjoyment, for learning.

Everything around us expands who we are

And our potential for love.

Even in the darkness we shine.

The night is never so dark that we cannot see.

Our eyes adjust to the darkness,

And even there we find a glimmer, a tiny light.

Even when the light is too bright, and we see too much,

We adjust.

We blink to take in only what we can.

We envision.

We see with our hearts.

The light is in us.

The light surrounds us.

I release the sound around me
To heal.
I focus on my breath.
I listen to the pulse of my heartbeat.
As I breathe in, I feel my healthy cells regenerate.
As I breathe out, I let pain leave me.
As I breathe in, I feel the warmth of my body as it heals.
As I breathe out, I rid myself of disease.
I continue to breathe … slowly.
I imagine myself in a restful place.
It can be cloudy or sunny, warm or chilly.
However I want it to be.
Someone touches my hand. It is the person who brings me comfort.
Now that I am in this comfortable place,
I can relax.
I keep breathing … in … out …
And now each breath carries me
Into wholeness.

CALM
Calm
calm
I collect myself. I pull inside.
The noise, the clutter, is external.
What is inside is real.
What is inside me is what I need to hear.
At my core, there is only one sound:
My heartbeat.
My.
Heartbeat.
My. Heart. Beat.
Unique. Solitary. Mine.
It sets my pace.
It is my pace.
My heartbeat gives me life.
My heartbeat brings me back to Source.
I hear what is really me.
I see what is really me.
I feel what is really me.
I know what is really me.
CALM
Calm
calm

YES!
That word works in any language.
¡Sí!
Yebo!
Oui!
Yes is truth.
Yes is humility.
Yes is strength.
Yes is peace.
Yes is calm.
Yes is surrender.
Yes transcends religion.
Yes is beyond spirituality.
Yes is transparent.
Yes is boundless.
Yes is expansive.
Yes is shareable.
Yes is contagious.
Yes is what we all want to say.
Yes is within us all.
Yes is clear and colorless.
Yes is on the surface,
In every crevice.
Yes is rewarding.
Yes is simple.
Yes.

Who am I willing to be?

Who am I?

I reach deep to answer the question.

I am not my job. I am not my house or my car or my clothes.

I am a person unlike any other, with a potential unlike any other.

I have a Purpose unlike any other.

After I am gone, when my body is gone, the spirit of my effort remains.

My impact, great or small, is long lasting.

Who am I willing to be? – *willing*

With that word – willing – I make a commitment. I say, "I will."

My willingness is my loving embrace of my talents and generosity.

Who am I willing to be – *to be*

I cannot be that which I am not.

I can only be who I am.

Through reflection, I learn who I am … I <u>live</u> who I am.

I give of who I am. I receive who I am. I am humbled by who I am.

Who am I willing to be?

There is only one answer.

Listen.

There it is.

Waiting for me to speak the words.

Who am I willing to be?

Tell me.

I am willing to release fear.

Fear is a fence,

A wall between my dreams and me,

A wall between reality and me.

When I release fear, I open the door to possibility.

When I release fear, I allow myself to see, to hear, to explore.

I release fear to make room for something new,
    something better.

There is a great reward for releasing fear.

The reward is freedom. The reward is possibility.

When I release one fear, all the other fears disintegrate.

When I free myself of one, I free myself of all fear.

It starts gently, as I say,

I am willing to release fear.

I am willing to release fear.

I am willing to release fear.

To let go of fear, I first have to fully acknowledge it.

What is this fear? What hold does it have on me?

When did it start? Where did I learn to be afraid?

Did someone tell me to be afraid? Or did I invent this fear?

What do I think I will lose?

As I release this fear, what is the worst that can happen?

When I release this fear, what is the best that can happen? What if I feel better?

What if I release this fear and nothing happens?

What hold does fear have on me? What could I do when I release it?

How might I be better, feel freer, feel less burden when I release fear?

What could be?

I focus on "what could be?" and fear starts to fade. It crumbles.

I focus on "what could be?" and potential starts to take hold.

I focus on "what could be?" and I see that I have planted something that will grow.

I see something wonderful beyond fear.

As I step away from fear, I see possibility. I see what can be.

As I step forward, I see something better for myself.

I am better than I've ever been.

I am willing.

I am willing to release fear.

Peace is all around me.
Within my circles of contact,
I share peace.
Every person has peace within.
I can see it in their eyes,
Behind the mask,
Behind the concerns of the day.
Everyone I see is
A being of peace,
A being filled with peace,
A being with whom
I can exchange peace.
I connect with people,
Eye to eye,
Peace to peace.
I see them.
They see me.
There is no need for words.
Peace speaks.

I accept that I can offer something to soothe another.

A hug is not always possible, so I offer a kind word.

Judgment is not useful, so I ask a question.

Ignoring is not the thing to do, so I smile.

I let the energy of my smile extend beyond my mouth.

I feel the smile start near my lips.

The formation of those facial muscles reminds me of happy times.

Happiness goes beyond my face.

As I feel my joy

My smile flows warmly into my arms and hands

Legs and feet

Through the core of my body

To the top of my head.

My smile has filled my body.

It glows, inside and out.

Those around me seem to notice the glow. They smile, too.

My smile is contagious.

How far can I extend my full-body smile?

Can I communicate it by phone? Is it visible on Zoom?

Does the cashier gently bag my groceries because she has caught the energy of my smile?

Let me see if I can share it with someone in another country.

Now that I know how far my smile can travel, I want to smile more often.

Now that I know how big my smile can be, I want to share it.

I accept that I can offer something that soothes another.

I offer the energy of my smile.

Hope. Light. Being.

I am a creator of hope.

I make it possible for all those around me to feel hope

By being hope. By exuding hope.

When I listen, as I speak,

I set an example of hope.

I model hope.

People see in me a possibility, a glimmer of light.

I let that light shine in me, through me, around me.

I know life can always be just a little better than it is right now.

I turn on my light so I can see where I'm going.

I am a ray of hope.

In my light, people find their way and their own hope.

The light shines in them.

This is how we live together in this world.

We share the hope. We share the light. We shine the light
for each other.

In that light, whether pale or bright, we can see.

In that light, we find hope.

The light grows. Hope grows. We grow.

Those around us feel hope grow in them.

We do this with each other.

For each other.

We are creators of hope.

This is where I am.

I am willing to release frustration.

I release what upsets me about a person or a situation.

I see that I am responsible for my emotions,

That frustration does not benefit me.

Before I can make room for better, brighter emotions,

I make room in my heart.

I make room in my mind.

I consider external factors ... only long enough to study my reactions.

Then I release my reactions.

I make space to bring patience into my life.

I make space to bring in compassion.

I make space to bring in empathy.

I look at people and situations as opportunities.

This is where I can love.

This is where I can understand.

This is where I connect.

This is where I am.

I am where I need to be.

What I see around me is what I need to see.

I take small steps.

Whether I stay at home or travel the world, I go slowly.

I am not in a hurry.

I take in what is in front of me.

I use all my senses.

I smell the food and plants and trees.

I see the colors of clothing and houses and landscape.

I see how people walk.

I hear the voices of birds and animals, of weather.

All these voices speak to me.

I taste flavors, individually and combined.

I savor the nourishment and the treats.

I feel the texture of a culture, of a society.

My attention to life comes easily.

I observe, and I reflect.

I have, around me, all that I need to have.

I am where I need to be.

My hand is open.
My open hand is more effective than a closed fist.
When my hand is open, I reach out. I connect.
When my hand is open, my mind and my heart are also open.
I ask more questions. I am able to hear the answers.
When my hand is open, I avoid judging others.
I don't tell them what I think.
When my hand is open, I am receiving.
I listen, because what they say is important.
When my hand is open, I understand.
I see where the lines of "what is important" intersect.
I see how we can travel together … work, play, live together …
Because my hand is open.

I listen. I say yes.

I listen as a way to separate the real from the contrived.

I listen to know what to keep.

But there is more.

I hear more.

There is a breeze that whistles through the trees.

There is the sound of rain, the silence of snow.

There is the song that comes from animals.

There is the rhythm that courses through my body.

I am comforted by these gentle, clear sounds.

Within, I hear something.

It's what I need to know, what I've been waiting for.

It is full. It is whole. It is complete.

Listen.

I have heard the wisdom, and I say yes.

I have heard the sweetness of possibility, and I say yes.

I have heard the sweet music of truth. I say yes.

No resistance. No argument.

My knowledge is complete.

My understanding is glorious.

There is nothing else. I have what I need.

I listen, and I say yes.

Peace is the goal.

Peace is the destination.

Love is the vehicle that takes us to peace.

I am the driver of that vehicle.

Peace only happens if I love.

On the road to peace, we all drive in the same direction.

We all go at the same pace.

We cannot beat each other to peace.

There is no prize for being the first one to get there.

We go together. We enjoy the ride.

And we cooperate; a collision would defeat our Purpose.

A pile-up would slow us down.

When one person forgets to love, we all miss out on peace.

Love. Cooperation. Patience. Compassion.

It's all easy when we have the same goal.

Peace is the goal, the destination.

Love is the vehicle that takes us there.

I look at myself in the mirror.

I reflect on what I see.

I identify my biases.

I see their origins.

I see how I normalized them.

I look deeper to see that my biases are not normal.

My biases are unfounded.

There is no scientific evidence for biases.

They do not serve me. I release them.

In their place, I adopt a practice of empathy.

Instead of thinking I am different from the rest,

I see how we are the same.

We have so much in common.

We have so much to offer each other.

I think of the ones who taught me bias,

And I have compassion for them.

I carry them with me until they can see for themselves.

I lead the way on the Path of Empathy.

I set the tone in what I say and what I do.

I make empathy a priority in my life.

I let everyone see how easy it can be.

We look at ourselves in the mirror.

We reflect on the goodness we see.

What is this heartbreak?

If life is to be lived in joy, why is there heartbreak?

Why is there sadness?

Why do we feel this crushing sorrow?

I do not know fair or unfair. It's not mine to say.

I do not know who deserves what. It's not mine to judge.

What I know is balance.

Balance is the equal distribution of circumstances above and below.

We have our times of sheer ecstasy,

And we have our days of sorrow.

I recognize this as the natural flow of life.

This is the natural rhythm of things.

When I feel joy, I appreciate it.

When I feel grief, I appreciate it, too.

Two halves make the whole. Yin and yang.

My acceptance of this flow humbles me.

My acceptance of this flow gives me hope.

Life is balanced.

I accept the balance in my life.

Mortal. Tragic.

The words were at opposite ends of the word search puzzle.

And that's where they should stay. At opposite ends.

I am mortal. I am not tragic.

Mortal means I will live and I will die.

I will live – fully! – until I die.

Tragic? No. Quite the opposite.

I am mortal, which allows me to be

Fortunate, lucky,

Healthy, hopeful,

Encouraging, delightful,

Joyful, pleasant, blessed.

I am mortal, with a limited time in this life …

And a lot to do.

I am mortal, and I share an energy that affects everyone around me.

This is my legacy. This is my very achievable legacy.

I am mortal. It is not a shortcoming.

It is my strength.

While I am here, I spread love and cheer and light.

I see the best in everyone.

Because I can. Because I choose. Because I am.

I am mortal. I have a deadline. I have an expiration date.

I live as if I might die. Because I will.

I am mortal.

And so I live!

The wisdom to know the difference.

Wisdom whispers to me,

Telling me what I can change … and what is out of my control.

I could ignore wisdom. I could push to change the unchangeable.

But I don't.

I prefer to focus my time and my energy on what I <u>can</u> change.

That's where the joy is! That's where I know I can succeed.

There are imposters who claim to be wisdom.

If I didn't know better, they would steer me in the wrong direction.

But I do know better.

I know wisdom.

Its presence is definite.

Its voice is clear.

Its vision is 20/20.

Every day, I listen for wisdom.

Every day, I hear its message.

Every day, I make a conscious choice to accept what I hear.

It takes awareness.

It takes humility.

I am aware of the gift that is in front of me.

The gift is wisdom.

I listen, and I say yes.

Peace is in me.
It is the heart of who I am.
No matter what happens around me,
I remember what lies within.
Peace is part of me.
God-given.
Always plentiful.
Peace is a
Single raindrop within a storm.
It is a moment alone.
A hummingbird on a sunny day.
The smile of a friend.
I take time for peace.
Every day,
Even in the last moment of my day,
Before I fall asleep,
Peace sets me free.
Peace is where I find myself.

The wind is not only external.

A gentle breeze gets my attention.

A wild wind worries me.

The movement of air on the outside reminds me of the unrest within.

There are days when leaves blow and branches fall,

And when it is over, I pick up the debris and move on.

Within me, there are days of gentle breeze and days of wild wind.

I recognize them. I feel their strength.

They pass.

I move on.

An occasional storm within does not change who I am.

It is simply an internal weather system.

It allows me to appreciate the pleasant days.

I can choose the kind of internal weather I prefer.

I become a wind whisperer.

I choose when to say, "That's enough now."

I pick up the debris.

I move on.

Give up? Keep going?

I can choose.

Which?

I collect information. I ask for feedback.

I consider options. I weigh choices.

I listen to my feelings.

Fear. Anger. Guilt. Freedom. Joy.

I take my time.

As I go to sleep at night, I remind myself,

"I don't know what to do right now, but I'll know in the morning."

And I do. The next morning, I know.

I always know.

The ritual of options is a way to calm myself until I hear my own pulse.

With my pulse, my internal rhythm,

I know what to do. I have the answer.

You have the answer.

Listen. Listen.

Listen to your internal rhythm. It always tells the truth.

It is clear.

You already know what to do.

How do I say what is in my heart and my soul?
How do I say what words cannot express?
Beyond thought. Beyond language.
Music might convey.
The best I can do is focus
On the song I hear,
The song I hold near.
And pass it on to you.
Here.
Hear.
Listen.
I give you my songs, and they become yours.
I tell you my thoughts, and they become yours.
I say to you my words, and they become yours.
I give you my heart.
Pass it on.

Stand where you are.

You don't have to move.

The place where you stand is yours.

Uniquely yours.

You have chosen it, and it has chosen you.

The place where you stand defines you.

Because of you, that place will never again be as it was

Before you.

It is your choice to stand where you are.

If you like where you are,

Stand where you are.

But

Know where you stand.

Your view from here is unparalleled.

If you stand on a hilltop, you see

All that is around you as an eagle sees.

If you stand in a hole, you might only see

A small patch of sky when the eagle flies by.

Know where you stand. Know your perspective.

How far you have come. How far you can go.

Where you stand makes a statement.

Where you stand is where you are just before

You choose to walk or run or fly.

Stand where you are.

Know where you stand.

Peace has a thousand arms.
It embraces me with love.
When I am lonely,
It holds me close.
Peace is a comfort.
It is a hug
Beyond human touch.
Peace is my connection to
That which is greater.
Invisible and indivisible,
Peace touches me.
Peace catches me when I fall.
Peace protects me.

I connect with those around me.

I take them into my heart as they pass by.

Trees. People. Animals.

Every living thing.

As I see, I accept.

As I accept, I love.

As I love, I feel a sense of appreciation.

For the shade of the tree.

For the knowledge of the people.

For the wisdom of the animals.

As I quietly express my thanks, I feel something change.

I feel a shift.

Is that tree a little taller?

Is that person a little nicer?

Does that animal look like she is smiling?

Or is it just me?

There will be those who say, No.
Those who tell me I can't.
I shouldn't. I don't know how.
I hear them. I consider their words.
And then *I* decide.
For who knows better than I?
And even if I can't or shouldn't or don't know how,
It is only temporary.
I can learn. I can overcome.
I can grow. I can be.
I can.
I can.
And when I do, I will look on those who said, No.
I will not judge them.
I will see their comments as their own opinions,
With no effect on me...
Except that they inspired me
To go farther, to reach higher,
To be more.
Because I can.
Because I am.

Sometimes I do not speak.
In my life, I have been loud.
Up until now.
I have been sarcastic,
Outspoken, quick of tongue,
Judgmental.
And often wrong.
Up until now.
Now, sometimes, I do not speak.
The world is not mine.
I share it with those whose voices are rising.
Those whose voices should be heard.
I make way for them.
I listen to them.
Sometimes I support them.
Other times, I ignore them, with respect.
I love them, but from a distance.
We travel this world together.
We all have something to say.
We all have something to hear.
We each have our own time.
To speak. To listen.
We each have our own time
To reflect.
Sometimes I do not speak.

I think of how we fight to get through these times.

How fear makes us fierce.

How adversity makes us warriors.

We keep going

Beyond what feels possible.

We keep pushing.

To get through another day.

I've become numb.

I'm not sure when.

The troubles built and built.

I cried a lot for a while, and then I didn't anymore.

Half hope – half surrender.

Admission that I don't know.

Understanding that my time is over.

In that admission – in that SUBmission – there is hope.

My sub-mission,

The mission that is one layer deeper.

Something I am called to do.

I listen.

I say yes.

We carry it with us.
All of it.
Every bit of our lives,
Plus the bits we pick up along the way.
We ignore. We dismiss. We override.
But it's all still there …
Until we release.
Some wounds are deep – we release what we can.
Some wounds are raw – we release what we can.
We let go in layers. A little bit at a time.
With time. With understanding.
With forgiveness. With empathy.
Instead of marching forward, we step lightly.
Instead of forcing and insisting, we move with respect.
Instead of shouting, we speak humbly.
Our experiences differ, but we share
Strength, delicacy, resilience.
We allow ourselves to continue,
For ourselves and for each other.
We see the load the others carry.
We help them where and when we can, as they do for us.
This is how we share the load.
This is how we travel together.

My load is not so heavy that I cannot help you with yours.

I am never too busy to see you.

I am never too deaf to listen to what you need.

We are never alone. It is energetically impossible.

In times of physical separation,

We are in the presence of each other.

When we cannot gather, we can still communicate.

When we cannot touch, we can still feel tenderness for each other.

When we cannot see each other,

We can see each other in ourselves.

I see you.

I hear you.

We are never alone.

A garden is a
Place of peace.
The flowers of gold and red,
Pink and purple.
The leaves that are
Every shade of green.
The tree that flourishes,
Protecting me,
Its leaves waving to me in the breeze.
The ivy that trails the walkway.
The soil,
Rich, moist, deep brown,
That sifts through my fingers
And gives these plants a home.
Vegetables so plentiful -
Enough for everyone.
The gentle flow of water,
Nurturing everything.
Hummingbirds.
Butterflies.
Worms. Honeybees.
A tiny green frog.
They all join me to
Celebrate this space of
Growth and abundance,
This cornucopia.
A garden is a place of peace.

People come and go.
The ones we love. The ones we will never know..
We are expected to adjust. And we do.
In time.
How we live the lessons
Is how we are remembered.
No one knows our names.
No one cares when we were born or died.
But some little nugget of wisdom,
Some tradition, some phrase,
Endures.
Some little thing we did or said
Becomes the pattern and fabric
Of those who come after.
We forget each other so quickly,
Yet our energy continues.
Energy is neither created nor destroyed.
It is what we are, who we are,
What we have always been, what we will always be.
Our energy speaks volumes,
And it will be heard for generations to come.
Make it good.

I focus on the sweetness of life.
Snuggles with loved ones,
Giggles, smiles, wagging tails.
Love shown and shared,
Nearby and over great distances.
The times change, traditions are updated,
Styles adjusted, allowances made.
Yet somehow we remain the same.
Our hearts still love.
We still want peace.
We still feel empathy.
We still give thanks for rain
And smile widely at the sun.
We still nod in acknowledgment of
Another dawn, another sunset.
And so it continues.
We love. We lose. We live.
We listen.
We are blessed.
We are grateful.
We focus on the sweetness of life.

It's quiet now.
The traffic has stopped.
It will return tomorrow.
The overnight sirens have ceased their howling.
Most people are asleep.
My job is to wake them
From their gentle rest
Into the reality of their day.
Each one is different
With unique desires, their own needs
(or what they think they need).
I am not their instructor, not their informer.
I am their companion.
I am the company they keep
As we discover the day together.
I hold their hands
As possibilities unfold.
Or collapse.
It's quiet now.
Until it isn't.
Until it is again.

When the mind becomes full,
The body absorbs the rest.
When the mind is troubled,
The body feels the impact.
I clear my mind of troubles
So the physical self can be strong.
I sustain a lightness,
Keeping touch with the present,
So my body can also feel light.
I maintain a mental smile
To keep a physical smile.
When a cloud enters my mind,
When darkness calls,
I ask what it has to offer.
Shade from the sun? Good!
A touch of rain? Welcome!
A bad mood? No, I don't need that.
I resume clarity. I enable light.
My mind is grateful.
My body thanks me.
And all is well.

Change
Happens slowly,
Then all at once.
Change
Comes
When we least expect it.
How much of it is welcomed?
How much of it is tolerated?
What do I accept?
What do I release?
What do I revise?
When do I move forward?
As I listen, the answers come.
As I hear, I connect. I understand.
I see change, a new order.
What seemed foreign becomes a part of me.
Change
Happens slowly. Then all at once.
And it will change again.
It is the flow.
It is the continuance.

Peace is where I go.

To escape.

To recharge.

To listen.

To learn.

To get in touch with myself.

Peace is not a place.

I don't need a ticket to get there.

I can stand right where I am

And find peace.

Peace is within me.

Peace is in my heart.

Available.

Reliable.

A tappable, ready resource.

All I need do is

Want peace.

I say its name.

It appears.

Peace prevails.

I see you "in the green."
Green means *go*.
It is the color of forward movement.
As I look around, I see the movement
Of people, of civilization,
Of time.
I see – and I accept –
That everything moves forward.
You are not who you were.
I am not who I was.
I see the good in us.
I see the good in how we have moved forward.
And if we misstep – when we misstep –
We can pause, assess, examine, explore
And move forward again.
It is good that we have reached this point.
I see the good in this moment.
I see the good in our progress.
I am open to possibility.
I am willing.
The light is green.
And we go …

You never know, I thought.
I never know.
I am so glad about what I don't know.
If I knew, I might worry or judge.
I don't know, so I stay in the present.
I enjoy where I am,
What I experience, who I know, what I have
Right now.
I release what I do not know.
I don't think about it.
It is out of my hands.
Out of my hands.
My hands are empty,
Free to create,
Free to hug.
My empty hands can give and receive.
It's out of my hands.
My hands are empty.
My heart is full.

Early science lesson:
Energy cannot be created or destroyed.
It continues.
Energy has no beginning or end.
It changes shape, but it goes on.
Always has been. Always will be.
Yet energy is so fragile, so malleable,
That my breath alters its course.
Energy is open to that change.
Energy does not resist change.
Energy accepts what happens.
Energy adjusts.
I see the effects of my words, my actions.
I see that I alter the world's energy
With everything I say and do.
I shape it and give it direction.
I also see that
Energy is flexible.
I learn to change with grace.
I learn to change without a fight.
I am energy.
Neither created nor destroyed.
I continue.

The truth should be easy to find.
More than the absence of lies,
The truth is love. It is open.
It is transparent.
Truth wants nothing.
Truth demands nothing, truth requires nothing.
Truth asks for nothing.
Ah, but what it gives!
Truth gives fully.
When we are blocked by fear and anger,
We don't hear the truth.
When we clear away the rubble,
The truth is evident.
It speaks. It is visible.
No bright lights. No special effects.
Truth speaks softly.
It is but a whisper.
Truth enters my being before I am aware.
I am filled with truth.
I am filled with love.
I am open.
I ask for nothing.
Truth is easy to find.

What am I hiding?

What is taking up space?

What is filling my time?

What fails to fulfill?

What leaves me empty?

And now ... I ask ...

What am I willing to release?

What can I let go?

I look to refresh and revive my being

By filling myself with different energy.

I start by releasing that which does not work.

What has grown old?

What is no longer useful?

I set it aside. With love.

I acknowledge and honor how I felt before,

And now I release it.

I look at it. I listen to it. I let it go.

As I release, I feel the space within.

The space invites fresh energy.

I make room for Purpose ... for meaning ...

I prepare for richness and fullness to enter.

I am open.

I am here.

I am love.

I do not know the meaning of the word *deserve.*
From a place of cruelty, people say,
"He deserved that."
From a place of fear and lack and defensiveness, they say,
"I don't deserve this."
Deserve.
The word is filled with judgment
Of myself and others.
"He should have less." "I should have more."
But the word means something else.
From Latin, "to devote oneself to."
I can work with that.
I devote myself to seeing the good in everyone.
I devote myself to seeing the good in myself.
When I devote myself,
I want the best for all.
I listen and look for the best of who we already are.
I see value. I hear potential.
I accept who we are.
They do not deserve less.
I do not deserve more.
We are perfect as we are.

I am surrounded by movement.
A breeze rustles branches of trees and
Blows through my hair.
People pass me on the street.
Cars drive by.
Water flows downstream,
Becoming waves in the ocean.
A bird glides overhead.
A friend waves.
Time flies.
Within movement,
There is something deeper.
There is peace.
I see it.
I feel it.
Peace is a moment, or
An hour, or
A lifetime.
Peace is a
Way of life.
Peace.
Be.
Still.

We do the best with what we have.

Our values. Our intelligence. Our material resources.

We do our best.

When I judge,

I do not see the best in them.

When I demand more, I do not acknowledge their value.

Instead, I ask myself and others

To rise up

By seeing the best.

When I see the best in people, they live up to it.

When I see the best in myself, I live up to it.

My high regard for everyone around me

Opens a space.

Through it, we can see each other.

We have room to love, honor, respect, acknowledge
each other.

I am doing the best with what I have.

I make it true every day.

As I do my best, I allow others to do their best.

It starts with me.

It starts with love.

We do the best with what we have.

Life is balance.

I feel a pull between the parts.

I decide how much.

How much of the spiritual realm?

How much of the material world?

How do I travel between spirituality and materialism?

Is the Path smooth between the two?

Or is it rocky, uneven?

I have what I need to balance as I walk this Path.

I see the balance of soul and mind,

Of spiritual and material.

I would not sacrifice either,

So I let them work together.

Spirituality and materialism are not enemies.

They are partners

In my life and in the world.

I have what I need to live in balance.

I have wisdom. I have common sense.

I have discernment. I have love.

I understand that all the pieces of life fit together.

This is the puzzle of life.

Life is balance.

I decide.

Life is balance.

I. Decide.

I am changing, but not yet changed.
I am complete, but not yet finished.
I've dropped out, but I haven't left.
I've surrendered, but I haven't quit.
What I feel is not who I am.
What I think is not what I know.
Where I go is not where I am.
Where I look is not what I see.
My best is not my highest.
My lowest is not my worst.
My latest is not my last.
I continue to explore.
I continue to grow.
I continue.

I release people.

Those who do not care.

Those who do not contact.

Those who tease and bully.

Those who are sarcastic.

Those who do not encourage.

Those who do not see my best.

I release them.

This is but a momentary loss.

The void they leave

Is soon filled

With lighter, kinder, more open

Souls.

I have moved from "fear of rejection"

To "encouragement of departure."

I see these farewells as

Part of my wisdom.

I love them from a distance

As I become more aware

Of better energetic matches.

As I become

Aware of myself.

Zebras in the dark.

The BBC posted a photo from Africa.

Three zebras crossing a road at night,

Lit only by auto headlights, one in each direction.

I drive to work in the middle of the night.

I've never seen a zebra.

Only coyotes, raccoons, skunks, cats, rats, wild turkeys.

A hawk once swooped so low she almost hit my windshield.

What else is out there that I haven't seen?

What is in the dark,

Invisible without headlights?

It's a metaphysical question.

What have I not seen because I am in the dark?

What internal headlight, in my spiritual toolbox, can help me to see?

In addition to the predators who lurk in the darkness,

There are beautiful creatures.

Creatures of every stripe.

I want to see them.

Sky,
Thy name is peace.
Whether bright or grey,
At night or in the light of day,
You teach me
There is no limit.
Earth,
Thy name is peace.
Red, brown, tan.
You teach me to stay grounded.
Water,
Thy name is peace.
In the form of rain or snow,
A mountain stream or a mighty ocean,
Or any storm that comes my way,
You teach me that
Nothing stays the same.
Circle of life,
Thy name is peace.
Babies are born.
Loved ones die.
From dust to dust,
You teach me to
Celebrate each moment.

I glide
With ease,
Effortlessly,
From one phase of my life to another.
I am grateful for all of it.
Pleasant memories.
Lessons that have shaped me.
Friends who have been around for many years.
New friends just making themselves known.
Places I have seen in my travels
And in my dreams.
All have been a combination of
Intention and manifested chance.
All are blessings.
The next phase looks different.
I remember to live with intention.
I remember that glitter is not essential.
I remember my Purpose.
I continue to define my Purpose.
I carefully consider my options.
I trust.
I trust.
I am grateful for all of it.

Take time for yourself.

You'd like a month.

You'll take a week.

Can you find an hour?

Just five minutes would help.

Close your eyes.

Breathe.

Remember who you are.

Reconnect with Source, by any name.

Take a whiff of your favorite fragrance.

Visualize your favorite landscape.

Listen to your favorite sound.

Go there.

As you return to this time and place,

Consider the value of a short escape.

Consider letting your mind travel when your body cannot.

You can hit the Refresh button any time.

You can reset in a few minutes.

It's there for you whenever you choose it.

Remember to take time for yourself.

The ones we forget to thank:
The drivers who make room for you
To merge into traffic.
The shoppers who let you check out first
Because you have only two items.
The people who pick up
Something you accidentally dropped.
The passersby who smile.
The people who see you.
We offer a quick *Thank You*
Then quickly forget their kindness.
These are the people to remember.
Their small gestures make the world
A better place.
We recall their generosity.
We continue it
By doing something small for the next person.
We ask for nothing in return.
It is enough to do something for someone else.
Maybe a lot of small things.
To honor the ones we forget to thank.

What can we learn from asking

A simple question:

How are you?

The response offers an abundance of information.

We look at the person who answers.

What is in their eyes?

How does the mouth tense up or relax?

We hear the person's voice as they answer.

Are they lively? Weary?

We hear the answer.

A quick, dismissive answer.

A pause to consider how much to reveal.

A deluge of emotions.

Or no answer ... which says so much.

We learn a lot by asking.

The more we ask, the more we learn.

About each other.

About ourselves.

What do you want to know?

What can we learn by asking a simple question?

Go ahead. Ask it.

How are you?

When I release judgment,
I can be at peace.
When I release anger,
I can be at peace.
When I release greed,
I can be at peace.
When I carefully, thoughtfully,
Reflect on my behavior …
When I consider how my thoughts
Affect my behavior …
I can clearly see what I can release.
I can easily lighten my psychic load.
When I release,
I make room for
Something better.
When I release,
I let in more
Light and love.
When I release,
I let in MORE.
I joyfully release,
And I enjoy the space I create.
I am at peace when I release.
I am at peace.

I listen to the sounds around me.

Traffic. Children. Machinery.

Wind through the trees.

Water in a stream.

I listen.

And then I zoom in.

I tighten my focus.

I listen for the spaces between the sounds.

I listen for the quiet spaces.

I focus on those tiny moments of quiet.

I focus on the quiet.

I focus on the sound of stillness.

In the stillness, I hear only

My heartbeat – the sound of my life.

The sound is consistent.

The sound is my own.

The sound is who I am,

Regardless of traffic, children, machinery.

The sound of my heartbeat comforts me.

The sound inspires me.

I listen for the quiet spaces.

In the stillness,

I hear who I am.

I take time to heal.
The body, the mind, the spirit
All need time to heal.
Healing any one of the three
Also benefits the other two.
To ignore my healing
Is to delay my healing.
I take time because the body wants to heal.
I allow my body to rest.
The mind wants to heal.
I allow it to rest.
The spirit wants to heal.
I allow it to rest.
I accept the good health of my body.
I accept the good health of my mind.
I accept the good health of my spirit.
Even when I don't think I have the time,
I take the time.
It is a gift I give to myself.
I take the time
To allow myself to heal.

I breathe.

I think.

I am at peace.

I watch.

I listen.

I feel peace.

I don't have to find peace.

It's here.

I love peace.

Peace loves me.

Peace surrounds me.

Peace feeds me.

With peace,

I see the best in all of us.

With peace,

I see the love we all share.

With peace,

I see that we are one.

I breathe.

I am.

I am at peace.

Before I shop for food, I take a moment.
I consider what I will buy.
It's not a shopping list.
It's an awareness
Of where the food originates,
Of who planted and tended and harvested it.
I think about who works in this store
So that I may have access to this food.
As I prepare this food, I take a moment.
I consider what I am making.
It's not a recipe.
It's an awareness
Of my actions
To prepare my body as well as
My sustenance.
As I consume food, I take a moment.
I consider what I am eating.
It's a prayer.
It's an acknowledgment.
Whether I eat for nutrition or for enjoyment,
Alone or with companions,
I am aware of my food.

This is atonement.

A reflection of my ill will toward others.

A considered review of my treatment of them.

Not dismissive or judgmental.

Not a few minutes, but

Whatever it takes.

When I have carefully looked at my errors,

I look at how I can atone.

What can I do to correct an error?

How can I make up for what I have done?

What can I do now to offset what I did then?

"Nothing" is not an answer.

There is always something I can do.

I can always do better.

Atonement reflects on the past

And resets now

To improve the future.

I accept this opportunity

To review my words and actions.

To create a better experience for all.

I reflect. I change.

This is atonement.

I release that which imprisons me.
What is in my power that I can let go?
I find my strength in knowing
That I can walk away from
Addiction, anger, self-pity, fear.
I find my Purpose in knowing
That whatever I do for myself
Affects all that is around me.
I find my Self in knowing
That my mind is powerful
Beyond what I've used so far.
I find my power in knowing
That I will not be imprisoned
By anyone or anything.
I find my spirit in knowing
That whatever you do to me,
My energy lives on.
My energy extends to all.
My energy gives inspiration.
I am not yours.
I live a life of service to all
By my own choice.
This is who I am.

I am a product of my past
And of my future.
How can that be?
How can I be the result of
Something that is yet to happen?
Everything I do today
Shapes the future.
Everything I say
Affects those around me
And shapes how they are
Today and in the future.
I am creating our future.
Now.
I am recreating and adjusting the past.
I am a product.
I am a producer
At the same time.
I am not hindered by anything.
I use it all.
I am a product of past and future
Because they are intertwined.

Rather than analyze,
I look.
Rather than judge,
I observe.
Rather than worry,
I consider.
Rather than speak out,
I reflect.
I learn from everything around me.
The sky, the breeze,
The trees and their leaves,
Animals, people
Land and sea.
Every being teaches me.
Every situation is a lesson.
I am a constant student.
I progress in my understanding,
I continue to learn.
I do my homework quietly
And gladly
So that I am a good lesson
For everyone.

Today I decide to be healthy.
Not everything is in my control.
I look for the ways I can make change
For the better.
How can I do better?
How can I be of service to
My physical body?
How can I add to the quality
Of my physical movement?
How can I add to the quality
Of my nutritional intake?
How can I add to the quality
Of the time I use to rest and be still?
How can I add to the quality
Of my entertainment?
How can I add to the quality
Of my learning?
I make choices that propel me.
I make choices that inspire me.
Today I decide to be healthy.
And I see how.

Peace is ours.
Ours to share.
We are equal when it comes to peace.
We all have the same allotment.
We all have the same opportunity to be peace.
When I see someone who
Might need a dose of peace,
I openly share mine.
When I need peace,
I willingly accept it from
Another generous soul.
When sharing peace,
I remember
I never have to ask.
Peace is instantaneously shared.
Peace is an unlimited resource.
There is enough peace for everyone.

Today I choose to make space.
When my Path is covered in rubble,
I cannot find my way.
When I clear it out,
I can move forward.
I clear my heart of bias.
I clear my mind of worry.
I clear my body of toxins.
I clear my finances of debt.
I clear my garden of dead plants.
I clear my closet of ill-fitting clothes.
I clear my life of people who are selfish.
I clear myself of selfish thoughts.
I clear away my judgment of myself and others.
I clear away
Dirt, grime, mold, clutter
From my physical and emotional space.
I carefully remove anything and everything
That does not work.
I take care of all that remains.
Today I choose to make space.
Today I choose to find my Path.

As I release negativity, I look ahead.

I question what is next.

I felt safe, blanketed in the clutter.

When it is gone, I feel exposed, unsure.

I worry about the future.

And then I remember:

I don't know.

I have never known.

All I can do is look at each new day.

I can see opportunity.

I can find promise and hope and love.

I feel a new kind of comfort.

I am free of that which confined me.

I have removed that which held me back.

I see myself in a new light.

At first, the light seems too bright,

But my eyes adjust.

I feel revitalized

As I emerge from the cave.

I stand in the open space

In wonder. In excitement.

I look forward, and

I feel safe.

When a box of cereal falls from the cupboard,
I am bothered by the disruption.
I have to stop and pick up the pieces.
I have to shop to replace the food.
When I clean my closet,
I am sad to get rid of clothes that
Don't fit and are worn out.
Those minor disruptions become treasured times.
I can replace the old items with
A fresh flavor,
A new color,
A different texture.
When I experience changes in
Career, friendships, family, finances, housing,
I understand the opportunity.
The loss leads to an opening.
The heartache opens something new.
What will I do with this opportunity?
How will I accept this change?
How will I make the most of this situation?
The little losses prepare me for the bigger ones.
I see that I am capable.
I see that I can do this.
And so ...
I do.

We are all imprisoned in some way.
I carefully look to see what holds me back.
I look at my own behavior.
How can I release what I do
And replace it with
A better way of being?
I look at people around me.
Are they all partners with me on this team?
In what ways can I improve
My relationships?
Are there relationships I should end?
I look at my physical surroundings.
Am I safe here?
Are there toxins that affect my health?
In what ways can I improve my environment?
I live with my eyes open to
The choices I can make.
I carefully look to see what holds me back.
I am willing to break the chains
That have locked me in.
I am willing to embrace freedom.
I choose to be free.

I am ready for a new acceptance.
I am willing to see myself in a new way.
I am willing to take the next step in my life.
I don't know what it is just yet, but
In some higher sense, I know exactly what to do.
I am not running away.
I meet my circumstances, face to face,
And I make good decisions.
I reach deep into myself for understanding.
I talk to those who see the best in me.
I reflect on my talents, my gifts,
What I have to share with the world.
In the time I have here, how can I use
What I have for the benefit of others?
I take small steps.
I stand on solid ground.
Yet I move forward.
The Path is mine. I take it.
I am ready.
I am willing to see who I am.
I am willing to take the next step.
I embrace my Path.

The circle of life surrounds me.
I watch as people celebrate and mourn,
As they grow up and grow old.
Humankind has never adjusted to loss.
Each death, each passing hits hard,
As if it has never happened before,
As if we are the first to endure
This deep grief.
We celebrate birth with some short memory,
Acting as if this little baby will live forever.
And yet it continues.
We ask for more than life can provide.
We are surprised when life ends.
Are we naïve?
Why do we so easily overlook what is to come?
This is hope,
The innocent belief that we will not age
Until it happens.
The fervent wish that we will not be old
Until we are.
Hope is why we get up every day.
Until we don't.
And so it continues.

Today I look closely at my addictions
And I choose which one to release.
I acknowledge that addictions can range from
Alcohol, drugs and gambling
To food, anger and gossip.
How many times a day do I reach for my phone?
That might be my addiction.
How often do I criticize?
That might be my addiction.
I identify my addictions.
I work to eliminate them.
It takes work. I know that. I am ready.
I am ready.
The small step I take today is
Acknowledgment.
I have an addiction.
The small step I take today is
Acknowledgment.
I am willing.
I am willing to release my addiction.
I acknowledge, and I am willing to release.
This is the small step
That opens the door to something better.
I am ready.

Peace is more.
More than the absence of war,
More than the absence of anxiety.
Peace is the
Continuation
Of what is natural.
The rhythm of a heartbeat,
My own internal music
Is peace.
And it's more.
The pattern of the ocean's flow
Is peace.
The sun. The clouds.
Peace.
It's more.
A breeze.
A random snowflake.
Peace.
Peace is me.
Peace is you.
Peace is all there is.

When I say I am willing to release,
I am vulnerable.
I don't know what is next.
I see a door, but I don't know what lies behind it.
My willingness to release includes trust.
I trust that releasing this one thing
Makes space for something better,
Even if I don't yet know what it is.
I don't know now, but I will.
I never know what is next,
Yet I am willing to find out.
I am willing to be vulnerable.
I am willing to allow opportunities to pop up.
This is part of the Path of Life.
I welcome the good that comes along my Path.
I trust that something wonderful lies ahead.
I don't yet know what it is, but
I will recognize it and embrace it when I see it.
Until then, I keep my eye on the Path
As I release
And make space for something better.

As a child, I feared the darkness.
I was afraid of what I could not see.
As an adult, I know how to
Look into the darkness.
I know how to retrain my eyes,
How to reset my vision.
I allow my mind to adjust.
I recognize shapes in the darkness.
My hearing becomes more sensitive.
I am more aware.
As I prepare for the next phase of my life,
I release my fear of the dark.
I have the wisdom to know
I can see what I need to see.
I sharpen my awareness
Until the light comes.
Because it does.
The light always comes.
The sun always follows the night.
I walk through this dark spot with my eyes wide open.
My senses, my inner wisdom
Get me through
Until the light comes.

I search each face for love.
And I find it!
In a smile. In a sparkling eye.
Each face of each person
Has the potential for love.
Sometimes they forget.
But when reminded, they love again.
I search my heart for love.
I don't always feel love.
Sometimes I forget.
But then I witness the love around me.
I hear laughter. I see smiles.
I see the sky.
I feel the Earth beneath me.
I am grounded and I feel love.
I feel love and it helps me to be grounded.
I love what is around me.
I love *who* is around me.
In this place of love,
Everything is light ... and bright.
I remind myself
To love.

What will I wear today?

What will I eat?

What Path will I walk?

I make many choices in a day.

Some are so simple. Some more complex.

Some are immediate. Some require time for research.

I choose to take authentic action.

I choose to take action that is considered.

I choose to live in a way that

Respects people, animals,

The environment, traditions.

I choose to live in such a way

That everything I do and say is beyond reproach.

I choose to live an authentic life.

Every part of my life is a choice.

Every part of my life can be authentic.

I make decisions that accentuate the respect I feel.

I make decisions that are considerate.

I consider every decision I make.

I take simple action.

I take complex action.

I choose to take authentic action.

As I take authentic action,
My heart is open.
I act and speak with love and respect.
When I meet someone who acts differently,
I do not judge.
Part of authentic action is love.
My love is a greater force than disagreement.
I love those who disagree.
I love those who stand in my way to stop me.
No one can make me less than I am.
Their actions reflect their authenticity.
My actions reflect my authenticity.
I love,
I bend,
Yet I remain
Authentic.
I see through eyes of love,
And so I am authentic.
I speak words that honor and love,
And so I am authentic.
I take action that is kind and respectful,
And so I am authentic.
In all ways,
I take authentic action.

My heart is open.

Today, everything I do will be filled with love.

I will smile. I will nod.

I will hold the elevator door for the last-minute arrival.

I will let the weary person sit.

I will lift up the person who needs hope.

Today, everything I say will be filled with love.

I will lavish everyone with compliments.

I will tell people I love them.

I will say, "Yes!"

Today, everything I hear will be filled with love.

I hear birds singing. I hear people laughing.

I hear music and the joy it brings.

Was that an insult? I didn't hear it.

My love does not hear offensive words.

I respond with love.

Today, everything I see will be filled with love.

The sky, whatever color, is beautiful.

People are beautiful.

Flowers. Trees. Tall buildings are amazing.

Everything I do, everything I say, all that I hear and see

Is filled with love.

Today and every day.

Peace.

Our natural state of being.

We think we can only have peace if

We escape traffic and technology.

But peace is bigger than that.

Peace is everywhere.

In the sound of wind.

In the flow of water.

In the view of a mountain, or a valley,

Or a forest, or a desert.

Peace is even

In the middle of

A busy intersection.

Peace is

Mine to embrace.

Wherever I am.

Peace surrounds me. Always.

Peace is a natural state of being.

I need only listen.

And accept.

Peace.

Love swells in my heart.

It is in my core.

The basis of who I am is love.

Sometimes it comes easily.

Sometimes I forget, and I have to remind myself.

I find it easier to love than to hate.

Love feels better.

As love flows from me, it is a shared entity.

I feel it. Others feel it. They pass it on.

Love is continuous.

Love flows in all directions.

Once I set my intention to love

It is easy.

When I see love as an authentic action,

It is easy.

I give love. I accept love.

I can always find something to love.

In everyone I see, in every place I go,

I can find something to love.

Love swells in me.

It is my core.

Love is the center of who I am.

When I love, there is no judgment.

When I love, there is no fear.

Fear suggests that someone has judged me, and I have reacted.

But there is no fear when I love.

Love can win the most hateful people.

I keep loving them until they feel it.

Love is a shield that protects me from offense.

Don't bother me with your hatred — I feel love.

Don't take my time with your bias — I spend my time on love.

Love softens the hardest hearts.

Love softens me when I need it.

Love is a tool to build, not a weapon to overcome.

Love is the basis for my authentic action.

Love is at the core of my spur-of-the-moment good deed.

Love is what inspires my long-range goals.

Love is what I give.

Love is what I receive.

Love is a circle.

What I give comes back to me.

I love authentically.

Love is in everything I do.

Where am I going?

I do not know.

I trust the Path.

I trust my wisdom.

I trust my guidance.

I catch glimpses along the journey

That tell me where I am.

That show my progress.

That remind me who I am.

I look. I listen. I love.

I see. I hear. I love.

I am clear on where I am.

I am willing to release in order to have freedom.

I am willing to accept so that I may have abundance.

I listen. I say yes. I surrender.

I choose to take authentic action.

This is my Path.

This is my journey.

I follow it. I share it.

I trust the Path.

I trust my wisdom.

I remember who I am.

I walk on.

We watch the world.
It's easy because of technology.
It's hard because there is so much going on.
I allow my heart to watch
As I relax my mind.
It is not my job to fix the world.
It is my job to have compassion.
By focusing on love,
I deliver a positive energy.
By focusing on empathy,
I never feel overwhelmed.
By focusing on compassion,
I send the kind of vibration
I would want to receive.
I watch the world,
And I increase my
Capacity for understanding.
I increase my
Capacity for generosity.
I allow my heart to be open.
I am one with the world.

Where I live,
Spring comes alive with color.
It is our most vibrant season.
Around the world,
People look to their own season of
Longer days and warmer temperatures.
Baby animals are born.
Flowers bloom.
Trees sprout fresh leaves.
We are refreshed.
Our hope is revived.
We celebrate.
The windows of our homes are open.
The windows of our hearts are open.
We turn our faces to the sky.
The showers drench the earth.
The sun warms us.
We touch the earth.
We connect with our environment.
We smell the change.
We marvel at the rainbow of pastels.
It doesn't last long.
We rejoice in our annual gift.

I am willing to release fear,
And when I do,
All that is left is happiness and love.
Happiness. Love.
From here, I can do anything.
I let myself fill with
Happiness and love.
It's easy.
It's so easy.
In every situation, I ask myself,
How can I express love?
In every situation, I ask myself,
How can I share happiness?
I have so much to give.
I am happy to share.
It takes very little effort on my part,
And it does so much for someone else.
Sharing doesn't deplete my supply —
It expands it.
When I share, we all have more.
I let myself be filled with
Happiness and love.

I am grateful for things that work.
I turn on the water faucet – it works.
I am hungry – there is food.
It's dark – I turn on the light.
I'm cold – I have a jacket.
I am surrounded by examples of genius.
The people who created these
Devices of my household
Have given a gift I take for granted.
In my home, at work, at school,
In and around my community,
My standard of living is enhanced
By simple, and essential, infrastructure.
I take time to see – really see –
My advantages.
I am grateful for everything that works.

Peace is a blessing.
Always available.
Transferrable.
Inexhaustible.
Peace is a retreat
Into the depths of who I am.
Peace is the emergence of who I am.
A whole being
Connected to the world.
I share peace with all humanity,
With all that is.
I absorb the bounty of the
Earth and sky,
And I return it all
In the form of peace.
Peace is solitude.
Yet I am never alone.
Peace is quiet.
Yet I know peace even in the fray.
Peace is attained.
Yet it is always in me.
Peace is mine though I share it.
In peace,
I have all I need and want.
Peace is a measure of my life.
I live in abundance, joy, good health
And peace.

I look closely.
I see.
I look at my behavior, my reactions,
My likes and dislikes.
Then I take another look.
To see.
I look at the people around me.
What do they need? How can I be of service?
Then I take a closer look.
To see.
I look at my community.
The people. What we have in common. How we interact.
Then I take a closer look.
To see.
I look at my environment. How I take care of Nature.
Then I take a closer look.
To see.
What do I see?
Examples of cooperation.
Examples of patience.
Of compassion.
I see examples of love.
I hadn't noticed them before.
They weren't evident. They weren't clear.
Or I wasn't clear. Then.
But now I look closely.
Now I see.

There is light in this darkness.
On a clear night,
I see the moon and stars.
On a cloudy night,
There is a glow in the sky
From lamps and street lights.
I value the light, in any form.
It shows me where I am going.
I also value the darkness.
Without it, we would have no rest.
Without darkness, I would be distracted by what I see.
Without darkness, I would not appreciate the light.
When it is dark,
I know light is coming.
The sun always rises again.
But for these few hours,
I see what I can in the darkness.
My eyes adjust.
It's good here.
It's magical.
It's sacred.
It's our world. Few people stop to appreciate it.
And right now, tonight,
The darkness is mine.
This is a precious time.
To enjoy.

Everything changed.
In one year, everything changed.
People died. People thrived.
People showed their true colors,
Some with love, some in fear.
We found our heroes.
We applauded them.
We found the bullies.
We held them accountable.
We saw things we never thought we'd see.
We saw what we never wanted to see.
We saw ... what we never wanted to admit.
We saw ourselves.
We saw ourselves in others.
We saw others in ourselves.
We saw our values.
We saw our potentials.
We saw our willingness.
There will not be another year
Like this in my lifetime.
Everything changed.
I saw who I am.
I learned how much I can love.

And the circle continues to turn.
Where were we a year ago?
Where will we be in another year?
We remember ... and we do not know.
We remember that we do not know.
I look at what is happening here ... now.
I focus on this moment.
This moment is filled with opportunity.
This moment is mine.
This moment is mine to share.
To connect. To be of service. To give.
To love. To show compassion.
I am one among many.
This moment is one among many.
If I move too quickly,
I become tangled in the gears.
By moving slowly, intentionally,
I see more of what is around me.
I can go forward in a way that has meaning.
My one small action means a lot.
Today. Now.
And the circle continues to turn.

What do you want from me?
What do you need from me?
Today I listen.
To those I know,
To those who enter my consciousness,
I listen.
To the grand sound of the world,
I listen.
To the still, small voice within me,
I listen.
I say yes.
I am always called to do what I can
Plus a little bit more.
When I think I can do no more, I say,
"What little bit can I do?"
I can always stretch a little more.
Even as I rest, I consider how I can serve.
What is asked of me is the same.
At the core, this is my Purpose.
To do what I do well.
To stretch.
To always do my best.
I listen ...
And I say YES.

I look at the influences in my life.
Some good, some not so good.
I reflect on my response to their influence.
Did I think they were correct? Did I ignore them?
How did I respond?
After time passed,
How did I adjust?
Did I continue to follow their lead?
Did I continue to learn from them?
How did they shape me?
When did I set out on my own
Path of influence?
When did I begin to influence those around me?
What is my responsibility?
How do I set a good example?
How do I lead?
How do I listen to those who follow?
Every leader must also listen and follow.
I am accountable.
I reflect on my responses to those who influence me.
I reflect on my impact on those around me.
I continue to learn.

When do I stop?

There have been moments when I've said,

"I've had enough."

When do I know it's time to leave?

I've said goodbye to friends, relatives, lovers, employers

Who were not a good match.

How do I know when?

It's a combination of Gut Feeling and Logical Thinking.

It's a cross between Can't Stand It and Better Opportunity.

It's because if I don't leave now, something bad might happen.

It's because if I leave now, I can do something better.

I've said hello to friends, relatives, lovers, employers

Who match my growth,

Who encourage my growth.

When?

How do I know when?

I know because I listen.

Listen to others. Listen to myself.

Adjust. Adapt. Measure the progress.

Be vulnerable.

Know there is a time to stop.

Be humble enough to know when.

Be courageous enough to know when.

I stop when it is time to stop.

Four walls.
Blue sky.
Still water.
A true heart.
I give myself
Permission
To feel peace.
I reach inside.
Beyond opinion,
Beyond thought,
Beyond memory.
I reach into myself
To touch peace,
To embrace peace,
To be peace.

Disappointment leads to grace.

I am sad.

I am angry.

I am afraid.

I wonder how I could have been better.

I wonder why it ended the way it did.

And why it ended at all.

I grieve and mourn.

I feel the loss of something I loved.

I thought it was my Purpose, but

It has been ripped away.

Now I am left to reinvent.

I am left to redefine.

My Purpose was not what I thought.

I feel empty.

That emptiness is my beginning.

The opening makes space for

A new version of Purpose.

I stand up. I run. I fly.

I make the most of this opportunity.

I rediscover my Purpose

With humility and grace.

When I take things personally,
I overlook a unique opportunity.
Everything that happens affects a community,
Not only an individual.
If I am offended, I do not consider
The needs of community,
Only my own needs.
I cannot be of service, or
Live in my Purpose,
When I only think of myself.
I reflect on my loss, and
I turn it into something bigger.
I make it my gift to the greater good.
I find a way to make it something better.
My Purpose includes community.
My Purpose includes service.
If I take this loss personally, I miss the point.
I focus on my community, not on myself.
I focus on what I can give, not on what I receive.
I focus on love.
I focus on release.
I do not take it personally.
I move forward in love.

Loss takes me to something else.
When my joy is stripped away,
When I feel a hurt or indignity,
It is my cue.
This is my opportunity.
Where I go will be different –
Not better or worse, just different –
And I will see what I have never seen.
My Path is clear.
My vision is clear.
My heart is open.
I have felt heartache, and it has led to
This place of being open.
I cry until I run out of tears.
Then I walk forward.
I do not need to see the Path
To know I am guided.
I just need to say Yes.
I am happy to say Yes.
I have no choice but to move forward.
And in this motion,
I find peace and joy.

On the Path I walked,
He came straight toward me.
Just before we collided,
He lifted to a branch above.
A Swainson's Hawk.
My totem.
What do you want me to know?
I always ask when I see one.
The answer:
Fly straight. Follow the Path.
Then watch from a good vantage point.
Sit until you've seen your surroundings.
Measure the distance, assess your position.
Review your priorities.
Know your strength.
Recognize your power.
You have vision and perspective.
You can do what no other can do.
Do you see it?
Use it. Do it. Be it.
Then fly to another and inspire that person.
You know your message.
Deliver.

Authentic action is an act of devotion.
Through my day, I do so many things automatically,
From locking the door of my home
To taking a route to work,
I take action without thinking.
An authentic action is one that is
Intentional – I pay attention to how I do it –
Humble – I offer it as my gift to my community.
My action might be simple or complex,
Still, I do it with love.
I act in alignment with my Purpose.
I care about what I do.
I use my talent and skill.
I think about what I do
And its effect on those around me.
I am considerate in what I do
Because the energy of my authenticity
Stays after I am gone.
I feel my responsibility to be an authentic person
And for everything I do.
My life is an act of devotion.

Stress takes its toll.

Adversity wears me down.

I raise my consciousness.

Troubles will come along.

Disappointments will occur.

I prepare my heart and my body to respond.

My strength is all-empowering.

My surrender is all-encompassing.

It takes both – strength and surrender –

To get through.

And I do. I get through.

Life's events do not drag me down.

They inspire me. They improve me.

They prepare me.

I become a better person.

When I fight, I fail.

When I surrender,

I feel the fullness of life.

I accept the rich blessings that are available.

Within my perception of stress and adversity,

There is an opportunity.

I say Yes.

I reflect on the concept of surrender.

When I surrender, I do not give up.

Instead, I move through.

I see what is around me.

I acknowledge the impact of the situation.

I consider where and how I may be of service.

I do what I can.

The rest I release to someone else.

I gracefully,

Graciously,

Gratefully

Walk forward.

Walk softly.

Sing gently,

Even if no one can hear.

Your efforts may not be noticed.

That's okay.

It's your peace,

On your terms.

As you need it.

As you find it.

As you make it so.

Walk peace.

Sing peace.

Be peace.

Peace is a leaf floating downstream,

Knowing the ocean awaits.

Peace is my reflection in the water,

Knowing I am

Where I need to be.

Peace is the wind.

No matter how hard it blows,

I know my Purpose.

Anxiety and worry are not my friends.
The energy I give them is a waste.
I am wiser to devote my time to
Efforts that are
Uplifting. Enlightening. Useful. Helpful.
Generous. Inspiring. Educational. Healthy.
When I take authentic action,
I clearly see what is fear-based
And what is worth my effort.
When I take authentic action,
I spend my money wisely.
When I take authentic action,
I improve my health.
When I take authentic action,
I do not judge myself or anyone else.
When I take authentic action,
I improve people's lives.
I am generous.
I am compassionate.
Everything I do
Comes back to me as authentic action.

An occasional meltdown offers value.
I was afraid yesterday.
My fear led to a small, emotional meltdown.
No one was hurt.
Only one person witnessed it.
When I saw it, I apologized, and
I cleaned up the spill.
Then I took authentic action.
Every time I feel that twinge of fear,
Every time I head toward a meltdown,
An opportunity arises.
If I seize the opportunity, I can
Ask questions, allay my fears,
Ask for help, discover a higher truth,
Find a better understanding of myself.
Before a meltdown hurts anyone,
I ask myself,
What is the fear I am experiencing?
Which of my beliefs has been challenged?
How can I tap into my inner wisdom?
When I answer these questions,
I move beyond meltdown.
I move into opportunity.
I move into authentic action.

I am conscious of sad changes
Without worrying about them.
I know my loved ones will be ill,
Yet while they are here,
I encourage them to live fully.
Our losses cause sadness.
They may be long in coming
Or catch us by surprise.
Losses will hurt.
I must mourn.
I cannot ignore my grief.
I am conscious of the effects of my loss.
I may be sad. Also angry, impatient.
I may want to make drastic changes.
Instead, I look within.
I sit quietly. I cry. I remember.
I recognize my pain is natural.
I sit with it.
I allow myself to move slowly as I grieve.
I take time.
I allow my grief to run its course.
I know it may take a while.
I wait.

We repeat patterns
Until we realize we don't have to.
We continue routines
Until we decide to stop.
We do what we've always done
Until we do something better.
We act the same
Until we have a reason to act differently.
Until now.
This moment – right now – we can choose to change.
I want to improve what I do.
I want to do more for the people around me.
Whatever I think of my life so far,
I know I can be better.
Starting now.
I know the choice is mine.
As soon as I break my pattern,
The Universe conspires in my favor.
I am ready.
I repeated my patterns
Until now.
Now I choose to change.

What is your name?
Not the name your parents gave you.
Or the name from your siblings or classmates.
What is the name the Universe calls you?
Listen.
The wind whispers your true name.
He Who Cares For Animals In Need.
She Who Feeds The Ones Who Are Hungry.
On the breath of the Universe,
You learn your Purpose.
From the voice of the stars,
You know who you are,
What you must do.
You don't have to think about it.
You don't have to wonder.
When you need to know,
The Universe will speak.
Pay attention. Listen.
That seat is reserved for you.
You are uniquely qualified
To do what is asked of you.
What is the name the Universe calls you?

The wind makes no sound
Until it meets resistance.
So it is with my soul.
It is only when I feel a lack
That my soul cries out.
When nothing stands in my way,
When there is no resistance,
I am quiet within.
When I know my blessings,
I am still.
When I stop thinking,
And know what I know,
I am at peace.
Anything else is resistance.
My soul is strong enough
To baffle the resistance.
My spirit lets the wind flow through.
I do not know the fight.
I only know the flow.
I only know that which is quiet,
That which is still.
The wind makes no sound.

We all walk the same Path,
Yet each experience is different.
One is hungry.
Another is tired.
Another is alone.
Another travels on another day.
Another is filled with joy.
We are all different
Moving along
Side by side.
Together.
Parallel.
Separate.
Simultaneous.
A variety of lives
On the same Path.
It is the Path that binds us.
It is the Path that we have in common.
It is the Path that unites us.
Without it,
We might not notice
There is no difference at all.

Outside, I see anger.
I stand before that anger, and
I smile at it.
Outside, I see fear.
I look at that fear, and
I comfort it.
The beasts become calm when
They see me.
Anger and fear
Have no effect on me.
I see them, but
I do not take them in.
I am filled with peace.
I am filled with compassion.
I observe the rest.
I acknowledge the rest.
I walk away,
Leaving fear and anger behind.
I walk forward.
I glide.
I float.
I ride on the shoulders of
Those who came before.
I am grateful.
I am at peace.

I ask myself
A lot of questions.
Where am I going?
What is my Purpose?
Am I doing the right thing?
Today, I stop to consider
Why my questions are about me.
Instead, I can ask
How can I reach you?
What do I have to offer you?
Still about me.
Try this:
What do you need?
Where are you?
What are your talents, your gifts?
What is your Purpose?
What do you teach?
What is your beauty?
Until I release "me,"
I cannot see you.
Or know your beauty.
Or love you.

My love is not mine.
The love I feel is yours.
When I concern myself
With the love I express,
It becomes selfish.
Not really love at all.
Love is not love until I remove myself
And see love as you do,
Through the eyes of the recipient.
Love is only effective
When love is received.
I have not loved
Until my love is felt by someone else.
So I change my focus
From what I feel
To what you feel.
Our energies merge,
Our love becomes
A singular thing.
The Purpose is the result.
My love is not mine.

In that split second,
So early in the morning,
A life ends.
We grieve its passing.
In the same moment,
On that blessed day,
A life begins.
We rejoice in its arrival.
The comings and goings
Continue.
They are not surprises,
Yet we are always surprised.
What a blessing to witness
Beginning.
What an honor to witness
Ending.
The moments by which
We are remembered.
Chiseled.
Researched.
The book-end moments
That say we were here.

Our spirits speak out
In times of need.
When I have felt connection
To another,
Nearby or far away,
I know the communication
Comes from within.
No need for spoken word.
We have reached each other
On a different plane.
When have you felt
The caress of one who is not there?
When have you heard
The voice of one who is far away?
When it happens, take note.
It is not your imagination.
It is not coincidence.
We can tap into our
Inner connection
When we want, if we want,
To hear our spirits speaking
In time of need.

At the time of death,
The spirit of the dying
Reaches out.
You may feel it.
As a thought or a recollection,
Someone may cross your mind.
A few days later, you discover that
It was the time of their passing.
You heard their spirit.
Some people never witness
The voice of spirit leaving a body.
Those who do may not recognize
The importance of the moment.
It is energy, it is spirit,
Moving out of a human body
Making itself known
In the Universe.
It is calling us to
Remember a person,
To be aware of a body's death,
To be aware of a spirit's immortality.
And so it continues.

The mirror adds light to the room.
It reflects the brightest part of Nature
And brings it into my space.
I do the same.
I imitate the mirror.
I find the best of what is around me.
I allow the light to penetrate.
I acknowledge the shadows, but
I do not focus on them.
The night's darkness is just
A rest time for the sun.
When it returns,
When its light is in my home,
When it is reflected in the mirror on my wall,
I love it even more.
I use the mirror as my model:
How can I add light to my environment?
How can I bring brightness to those around me?
How can I illuminate?
How can I shed light?
How can I reflect the light and
Bring it into my space?

My blessings exceed all else.
Sometimes I closely examine them.
The details are clear.
At other times, I simply lump them
Into the giant category –
"Blessings" –
To identify their common theme.
But
There is nothing common about blessings.
Each is unique.
Each is magical.
Each is miraculous.
Each is mine
To enjoy,
To appreciate.
Each blessing goes beyond
My capacity for explanation.
Each blessing is bigger than
My ability to express my feelings.
There are so many.
I am grateful for each one.
I am astonished by each one.
My blessings exceed all else.

Don't forget who you are.
The voice of a friend
Standing in my doorway.
I had tried to ignore, to forget, to rationalize,
But the voice brought me back.
I remember who I am.
I remember
I am peace.
I close my eyes.
I take in a long, deep breath.
I let it out until I am empty.
That is the end of my unrest.
My next breath brings in calm.
It brings in clarity.
It brings in love.
I am calm.
I am clarity.
I am love.
I remember who I am.
I am peace.

I look into the Metaphysical Mirror
To see who I am.
There is no criticism in a mirror.
There is only observation.
Attention.
Acknowledgment.
How I got here is not important, but still,
It helps to know.
What I see in the Metaphysical Mirror is
The truth of my being.
Whether I call it
Soul or Heart or Core,
It is who I am.
It is my basis AND my potential.
It is where I've been,
Where I'm going,
Where I am.
The Metaphysical Mirror
Is my vehicle
From my outer being
To my inner true self.

In the mirror, I see
Light reflected.
The light comes from outside my window
And reflects in the glass.
The light comes from within me
And radiates outward.
The people who see darkness in me
Are seeing their own darkness.
The people who see light in me
See their own light.
Likewise, what I see in someone else
Is a reflection of who I am.
I am at my best when
I look for light in everyone.
I am at my best when
I shine my light upon everyone.
We can see in the dark, but
Our vision is clearest
In the light.
I share the light I know.
And in the mirror, I see
Light reflected.

My love isn't complete love until
It comes back to me.
When I express love,
Does it reach another person?
If not, is it really love?
Is my expression of love sufficient
If it does not have a recipient?
When my love reaches you,
It is complete.
When my love reaches you,
You return it.
You reflect it.
It comes back to me.
Love expressed, but not received,
Has not fulfilled its potential.
My goal, as a loving person, is to
Look for the love in others, to
Be open to their love, to
Allow them to love me.
I become a willing participant of love
So that love comes full circle.
I feel love. I accept love. I return love.
I forward that love to the next person.
When my love reaches you, and you reflect it,
The circle of love is complete.

My focus sets a tone.
A coach used to say,
"What if it isn't hard?"
He knew that a fresh attitude
Changes everything.
So I look closely.
Is it really hard?
How can I make it easier?
How can my words
Change my perspective?
How can my perspective
Improve my condition?
How can I ask questions that
Elicit a positive answer?
How can I take action that
Leads to a positive outcome?
Some things are hard.
Some things seem hard
Until we make them easier.
Some things were hard
Up until now.
My focus sets a tone.
My focus changes everything.

My words have power.

What I say can be calming.

The choice is mine.

What effect do I want to have?

How do I choose to influence those around me?

How do I want to be?

When I do not feel cheerful and bright,

How do I shift to something lighter?

How do I shift to something better?

I choose my mood.

Outside influences try to invade, but

I am the one who decides my perspective.

I decide to offer compliments.

I decide to provide encouragement.

I decide to see the best in people.

I decide to see the best in myself.

I decide to see something good

In every situation.

I use my words for the greatest good.

I choose my words with love.

My words have power.

Today I do something for someone who cannot.

Donate blood.

Donate books.

Donate clothes.

Donate shoes.

Play with dogs at the local animal shelter.

Serve meals at the local people shelter.

Collect food for a food bank.

Play music at a senior center.

Put up holiday decorations for a neighbor.

Mow a lawn.

Rake leaves.

Empty gutters.

Wash windows.

Deliver a meal.

Wash a car.

Take out the garbage.

Water the indoor plants.

Water the outdoor garden.

Today I do something for someone who cannot.

I look for ways to be of service.

I give from the heart.

We honor people's lives
By allowing their legacy.
We see the good in people.
We feel the good they do.
We thank them.
We tell other people about them.
We hail them.
Some are famous. Some are not.
Even the ones with statues
Are eventually forgotten.
But what they did,
Good or bad,
Lives on.
It's a different kind of afterlife.
Not all of my energy is good, but
When I consider that the
Essence of my character
Will last
Forever
I want to be a better person.
They will forget who I am, but
I want to leave behind
A lifetime of
Positive energy.

To everything, there is a season.
This is the season to stand.
Some stand in defiance.
Some stand to make their point.
Some stand to avoid falling to the ground.
Some stand to reach higher.
Some stand to be seen.
Some stand to make their voices heard.
I stand
Here.
I stand in my own space.
I stand with my feet
Connected to the good Earth.
I stand with my face exposed
To the sun,
To the rain.
I stand with
My arms spread wide and
My hands open.
I stand in peace.
This is the season for peace.

Time shows itself in perspective.

As children, it seems forever before we grow old.

Some days seem to last forever.

We have all the time in the world.

Later, as we age,

Time is fleeting.

We thought we would have more time.

Life is short.

Time shows itself in perspective.

We think time is on our side, but

In the big picture,

Our lives last only an instant.

How am I spending that instant?

With love? With compassion?

In anger? In spite?

In pursuit of money?

In pursuit of fame?

Honoring others?

We can choose how we live.

We can choose how we spend our days.

If we wait, it will be over.

Time shows itself in perspective.

I do not take offense.
There are people who love to hurl insults.
There are people who speak without thinking.
I choose a different way.
I choose to speak from a place of
Love, thoughtfulness, compassion.
I do not speak insults,
Nor do I receive them.
I hear the words directed at me, but
I do not absorb them.
I am aware of the slurs.
I do not accept them.
I do not make them my own.
Those who hate
Cannot shed their hatred on me.
My armor is strong.
My shield is up.
I neither sling arrows
Nor suffer from them.
I step aside.
I choose a different way.
I do not take offense.

I celebrate
The big decisions in my life.
I honor
The small ones.
With every choice I make,
I feel the vibrancy
Of my awareness.
I am aware of the gift
To discern my options.
To recognize possibilities.
To make good choices.
Even on days when I don't feel wise,
I recognize the gift of wisdom.
I use it to make good choices,
To improve on my previous choices.
My choices affect everyone.
My decisions are my gift to everyone.
I choose wisely for the benefit of everyone.
I celebrate
The decisions I make.
I recognize and honor
All my choices.

I know when to speak.
To defend someone.
To compliment someone.
To engage someone who is shy.
There are times when what I say
Adds to the fabric of the world.
In those times, my words flow
With an eloquence that comes through me.
From beyond me.
When it is time for me to speak,
I am a conduit.
I also know when to be quiet.
My voice is not always needed.
So I listen.
To hear other voices.
To hear their wisdom
When they are conduits.
I know when to speak.
I know when to listen.
Giving. Receiving.
Communicating.

Today I look.

I see where I am.

I see the walls.

The floor. The ceiling.

I see the sky.

The ground.

The buildings.

Homes and businesses.

There are people.

I see them.

Their expressions, their moods.

I see animals.

I see vehicles.

I see trees and plants.

I see the light

And the shadows it makes.

I see darkness.

I see possibility.

My eyes are open.

Today I look.

I see where I am.

I see myself.

Today I listen.
I hear where I am.
I start with my breath.
Every breath is a gift.
I listen to it, however quiet.
I hear other sounds,
The breath of those around me.
I hear a car, a bus, a train.
I hear children, laughing.
Other people, working.
They are saying, "Hello."
I hear a bird.
A dog barking.
I hear rain, splashing.
A breeze in the trees.
I hear the sounds of industry.
I hear the sounds of wilderness.
And in it all,
I hear …
Quiet.
Today I listen.
I hear where I am.

Today I use my sense of smell.
I take in my surroundings.
The places I sit and walk
Have unique aromas.
My home smells of
A meal,
Laundry detergent,
This morning's coffee.
Outside I smell
Elements of Nature –
The rain has a smell.
The hot sun on pavement has a smell.
The crisp winter air has a smell.
Other smells come from
Metal and exhaust in passing vehicles,
Food cooking in a restaurant,
Wood smoke from a fireplace,
Steam from a vent in the street,
Roasted peanuts from a vendor,
Flowers.
All fragrances,
Pleasant and unpleasant,
Reach my consciousness.
This is where I am.

Today I pay attention
To what I say.
My words reflect where I am.
I notice how I greet people,
Those I know, those I haven't met.
I hear how I speak
When I want something to be done.
I notice how I ask questions.
I notice how I answer questions.
I pay attention to the tone of my voice –
Patient, angry, curious, playful, stern.
I hear the words I choose –
Gentle, demeaning, complimentary, warm.
I notice whether I speak
Quickly or slowly,
Loudly or softly.
Do I talk to children?
Do I talk to animals?
Do I talk to myself?
How do I speak?
My verbal communication
Reflects where I am.
I pay attention to my words.

Today I feel.
I notice
My sense of touch.
The air on my face
Tells me warm or cool,
Humid or dry.
The fabric of my clothing
Has a texture,
Snuggly or coarse.
The steering wheel,
The pole on the bus,
The handle on the stairway.
A quarter in my pocket.
A dollar bill in my pocket.
A sandwich in my hands.
An ice cream cone.
The fur of an animal I pet.
The skin of a person.
My own skin.
My sense of touch
Connects me.
Today I notice what I touch.

Today I look at
What I have to offer.
To my family,
To my community,
To my profession.
What are the skills
And talents
I can offer?
I look at what I can
Give to others
Without depleting myself.
I look at how I can enrich people's lives.
My presence is my power.
My power is my gift.
I use it.
I share it.
It is not mine, but ours.
I am responsible.
I am accountable.
I look at what I have
To give.

Peace is recognition.
Peace is acknowledgment
Of everyone.
Peace is feeling the pain of all people
So that we can help them to heal.
Peace is having my eyes open
So that all can see.
Peace is allowing all emotions,
Letting them flow.
Peace is the prayer I offer
For anyone too weary to pray.
Peace is the beacon I hold
To light our way.
Peace is the one gift
I can give.

My voice remains calm.
Before I speak,
I make sure
I have something to say.
We don't need more empty words.
We don't benefit from chatter.
My voice remains clear.
I choose my words.
My meaning is clear.
My strength is clear.
My message is clear.
My voice remains strong.
I speak to one person,
Knowing that many will hear.
My energy
Moves the words along.
They float on the air until
They reach the right ears.
My voice is mine, yet
It is the voice of many.
Calm. Clear. Strong.
Shared.

That which is lost
May be found
Or may be forgotten.
We remember
With love
The things, places, people
That matter.
Through us
They live on.
In us, they live on.
When we look deeply,
We find what we lost.
If it matters.
Our loss reminds us that
Life is impermanent.
The moment passes.
The memories remain.
When the memory passes,
The energy remains.
That which is lost
May be found
Living in us.

This is how we love:
In everyone, I see
One good thing.
Just for today.
Even with people I don't like,
I can find one good thing.
Then I sit with that for a while.
Tomorrow I will look
At another person
And find one good thing.
Another the day after that.
Before long,
I will see
ONE GOOD THING
About everyone,
And that is a step
In the right direction.
I will love
The one good thing
I see in everyone.
One good thing at a time.
This is how we love.

Look. The answer is there.
Know where you are
So that you will
Know where you are going.
Track your progress.
Think of your life
As a journey on a map.
Are there hills to climb?
Are there streams to cross?
Is there heavy traffic,
Interference or companionship?
Your journey is not measured
In miles, but
In observation.
If you stay in one place, physically,
See the place
With wonder and awe.
You have made progress.
The soul travels even when
The body sits still.
Track your progress.
Know where you are.

The soul travels even when
The body sits still.
My mind takes me through
A tour of the Universe,
One stop at a time.
I decide whether to stay
Or keep moving.
The Universe is made up of
Villages, neighborhoods,
Each one inviting in its own way.
Many will appeal.
A few will feel like home.
Escape. Explore.
Here, I am loved.
Here, I love.
I recognize why I am here.
I see what I can do.
I see who I can be.
I see who I am.
My mind, my heart, my soul travel.
My body is still
Until I find my home.

Peace is in the interlocking threads of life.
The perfect braid of silver and gold
Woven,
Plaited together.
Peace is the fabric of who we are,
The weft and warp of our ups and downs.
Peace is in the varied greens of a grassy field
The reds of falling leaves
The shades of white in a snowdrift
The pastels of spring.
Peace is in the colors that are
Unique to every season.
Peace colors our world.
We see peace wherever we look.

There is hope.
Mostly.
We continue to look for
Something better.
Peace is in the fabric of who we are.
We do not have to know
What it is, exactly.
We do not need a precise vision.
As often as
Hope is clear,
It is just as often vague, indistinct.
Hope's job is to be
Different for everyone.
Hope's job is to
Wake us up,
Inspire us.
We continue to look for
Something better.
For ourselves, for everyone.
There is always hope.

What is it today?
I go to my news sources
With great anticipation.
I know I will find
The good in people.
I know I will find
A reason to hope.
People always help people.
I do. You do.
Around the globe,
It is happening.
I look beyond the top layer
Into the troubled spots.
I dig deep,
My eyes wide open.
And there they are -
Good people
Doing good things.
What do I see today?
The good in people.

Purpose.
Empathy.
Early in my day
The words shout out:
Here we are!
Use us!
After a few hours,
The debris of the day covers these words.
But that debris
Is not reality.
I dust off my Purpose.
I dust off my Empathy.
As I take them off the shelf,
They are not decorations.
They are meant to be used.
By me.
For you.
They are speaking:
Purpose!
Empathy!
Use us!

I feel anxiety.
I see where I am.
I feel strain and weight
From the pressure.
It might wear me down.
I look closer.
I see that some of the strain
Is self-imposed.
I see that some of the pressure
I have put on myself.
I see that some of the anxiety
Can be released.
I sit with the concept of
Release.
I am willing to let go
In small pieces.
I am willing to let go
At my own pace.
I am willing to let go
Of the pressure.
I release anxiety.
I see where I am.
I see who I am.

I feel relief.
I see where I am.
I enjoy the feeling of
A weight lifted.
I enjoy the feeling of
Joy, calm …
Absence of worry.
When my worries leave,
I have open space within
For something better,
Something bigger,
Something joyful.
I enjoy this sense of space
Between anxiety and joy.
I call it Relief.
I call it Possibility.
I call it an Opening.
I don't have to fill the space.
It will fill itself
With something good.
I feel relief.
I see where I am.

I feel joy.

I see where I am.

I see the source of

My joy.

I see the depth of

My joy.

I see what I can do with

My joy.

I see that I can call up

My joy.

On demand.

I choose to repeat my joy.

I know there is balance.

I know other emotions will try to block

My joy.

This joy is mine.

I know where to find it.

I know how to nurture it.

I know how to make the most of it.

I feel joy.

I see where I am.

I see who I am.

My location changes.

My work life changes.

My family changes.

I see who I am.

I make choices.

I release what doesn't work.

I accept what does work.

I see who I am.

I weigh the events in my life.

I expect the unexpected

I meet each day because

I see who I am.

I make adjustments so I can love who I am.

I love what I see in others because

I love who I am.

I understand the flow of life and

The turning of the world

Because I love who I am.

My heart is open.

I see who I am.

After the shouting,

There is peace.

After the fires,

There is peace.

After the famine, there is peace.

Whatever you feel now,

Peace will come.

Peace always comes.

Peace is so quiet

We forget it's there

In the corner of the room,

In the corner of our hearts.

We cover it up.

We ignore it.

We lose it sometimes,

With the car keys and the orphaned sock.

But peace never leaves.

It is always with us,

Filled with possibility.

It waits for us.

And when we are ready,

It hugs us.

It shines.

It nourishes us.

Peace never dies.

Peace is always here.

I trust others because
I trust myself.
I am not afraid because
I trust myself.
I make choices.
I review my choices.
I adjust my choices.
I accept my choices.
I trust myself, and
I trust something higher.
I see the choices of other people.
I review.
I adjust.
I accept.
I understand.
I encourage.
I see.
I listen.
I relate.
I love.
I trust.
I trust others because
I trust myself and
Something greater.

In every person,
I find one good thing.
That is my promise.
That is how I love.
I find one good thing.
Sometimes it is easy.
A smile, a twinkle of an eye.
It is obvious.
Sometimes I have to look hard
To find one good thing.
And it is there.
It is always there.
One good thing is
Waiting for me to find it.
I cannot fulfill my promise
Until I find
One good thing.
After I find one good thing,
I find another and another.
In every person
I find at least one good thing.
Promise kept.

Now I live on as a poem.
It is what has become of me.
It is what I have allowed myself to be.
I wasn't always a poem.
I was
Popular
Attractive
Comfortable
Smart
Maybe even
Respected.
I was
Tall
Slim.
All of that is gone.
Now only my energy remains.
I am my essence.
I am on the breeze.
I am all around you.
I am your conscience.
My Purpose is in these words.
Live a poetic life.

Anger is not poetic.
Poetry is not for that expression.
Poetic thoughts are kind and gentle,
A way to figure things out.
It is how we explain
What we see in the sky.
It is how we sort through love.
Wonder. Hope.
Poetry is how we reveal
Our dreams. Desires
That would never otherwise
See the light of day.
Poetry is a gift.
A curse.
A blessing.
An invitation.
A benediction.
I count the syllables
Before my next breath.
I write to read.
I speak the words.
Poetry is a prayer,
A meditation.
Anger must wait another day.

My words are here.

For now.

Waiting to be read.

On a screen. For now.

On paper. For now.

Waiting to be shared.

I speak words that are

My own. Often.

Of other people. Rarely.

I wonder what is left

For me to say

After I have said

The words given to me.

We are all told what to say.

The art

Is in the delivery.

I make the words my own

In the way I say them.

I bring them to life.

It is a conversation

Between One Person and me.

One sided.

Double sided.

My words are here.

Dreaming of faraway lands.
Friends moving.
Family traveling.
What I find abroad enriches
What I have at home.
I expand my appreciation
Of architecture,
Art, resources.
Let's go!
Let's come back
To expand on what we have.
Travel adds flavor
To the life I already live.
To breathe the air,
To take in the aromas,
To see the colors,
To observe the traditions,
To appreciate the culture.
Dreaming of faraway lands,
I see what I have,
And I grow.

Peace is a sound:
Kids at play.
Peace is a sight:
A flower. A tree.
Peace is a taste:
A morsel that rolls around the tongue.
Peace is a smell:
Any aroma that makes you smile.
Peace is a touch:
Warm or cool,
Furry or human.
Peace is a word:
Say it.
Often.
We know the
Wisdom in our senses,
And we know peace.

I feel lost at times.

Flailing. Groping.

The moment always passes,

But until it does, I doubt everything.

Then it lifts,

Thanks to my own creativity,

Thanks to my own ingenuity.

I look for the lift.

I see the encouragement.

I feel the inspiration.

My fear flies again.

In and out of certainty,

I recognize how the moods pass.

I acknowledge the ebb and flow.

The outcome is wisdom.

Always.

Certainty + uncertainty = wisdom.

Light + dark = a day.

One rolls into the other.

One cannot be without the other.

The moment always passes.

And so it goes.

On some days, I am organized.
On other days,
The Universe has its own plan.
The smoothest way through
Is to listen.
The greatest joy comes
In cooperation.
I defer to the greater plan.
I acknowledge something
Larger than myself.
I understand that my plan
Must give way to a greater plan.
This admission is humbling.
I am not in control.
I trust what is happening around me.
It seems chaotic.
Yet I know all of this
Leads us forward.
My current experience is what I need.
My current experience educates me,
Propels me, inspires me.
The Universe has its own plan.
The smoothest way through
Is to listen.

I might be overthinking.
When I think too much,
Overanalyze,
Worry,
It is a sign of my anxiety, fear, lack of control.
It usually means I have lost
My connection
To that which is important,
That my mind is idly finding useless ways to stay busy
Because it has temporarily
Detached from my heart.
I reconnect with
My heart.
I stop overthinking.
I reconnect with my Purpose.
I contribute to my community.
I reconnect with what is important.
I think only when necessary.

I lost faith in someone
Who said he would always be there for me.
But wasn't.
Or was he?
Did he let me down?
Or did I lose faith
In myself
And hold him accountable?
The lesson is clarity.
Look at what is.
What really is.
Be truthful.
Maybe I am the only one who will know, but
My energy circulates.
I can spread truth,
Or I can spread a lie I've told myself.
I'd rather spread truth.
I must be true to myself before
I can be true to anyone else.
I found faith in myself.

It is time to release.
I have tried for years to make it right.
I will not give up.
I will work at it again.
We all make choices.
I want to choose a higher road.
Compassion – because I sense
There is more to it than I know.
Empathy – as I would have others
Do unto me.
I choose to be helpful.
I choose to
Be a guide.
I choose to
Acknowledge everyone around me.
I clear the way for their success,
And I applaud them.
I cannot fix. I cannot save.
I can only work with.
That is my choice.
I am ready to release.

I am moving into
A new phase of my life.
It is time for me to be
Useful,
Purposeful
In a new way.
What can I offer?
How can I be a friend?
Is it what I say?
Or is it how I listen?
Is it how I excel?
Or is it how I make others look good?
As much as I love to be on stage,
There may be
A source of greater satisfaction.
I release my ego
For the greater good.
I unleash my potential for Purpose.
My energy is shifting.
I am in a new phase.
It is time
For me to be.

Packages on the doorstep.
Lights on the houses.
Preparations for the holidays.
Decorations everywhere.
How do you decorate?
How do you convey
The message of the season?
How do you create
Continuity
Between the happenings of the world and
What is possible in your heart?
How do you express the peace that can be?
What do you sing
From the mountaintop?
Let peace carry you.
Let peace define you.
Let peace be a comfort,
A blanket that caresses.
Feel the deep and resounding
Peace of this season.
Take it with you into
Seasons to come.
Wear peace.
Decorate with peace.
Be peace.

I already know what to do.

I've thought it through.

I've worried about it.

I've researched it.

Those efforts confirm what

I already know.

We have the answers we need.

Some of them have not yet

Bubbled up to the surface.

The timing is not right, or

We want to consider all options.

As I look within,

I understand that

I have the answer.

Sometimes my worry causes me to ignore

What I know.

Sometimes my search for answers causes me to ignore

What is

Right in front of me.

I take the time to go within.

I make the time to

Connect with the answers.

I confirm that

I already know what to do.

Every day is fresh and new.
I look back to a week ago,
An eternity ago,
And yet an instant ago.
How did so much change?
How do I grasp what has happened?
I don't.
I take remnants of the past,
I leave the rest behind.
I have a selective memory,
I save what I want to remember.
I absorb what I need to recall.
The rest floats away.
The rest serves no Purpose,
So I let it go.
The parts I save are precious.
I look for their value.
My memories teach me.
My past guides me.
Now I move forward.
Every day is fresh and new.

Take time for calm.

So much is asked of us.

Just pause.

Reconsider.

I ask so much of those around me.

How can I hold back?

Just pause.

Reconsider.

We are given opportunities to

Slow down.

I choose to take the opportunity.

I don't give in to the hype.

I don't need to be in constant motion.

My activity is balanced with rest.

I choose to be in balance.

I say no to constant disruptions.

I choose to be in balance.

I ask those around me to slow down.

I choose to be among calm people.

I find comfort in quiet time.

I look within.

Just pause.

Reconsider.

Take time for calm.

The choice is mine.
At a very deep level,
In my core,
I decide my options.
I choose where I live.
I choose where I work.
I choose my friends.
I choose the people around me.
I choose the highest of these:
I choose to live
Where I am safe.
I choose to work
Where I am respected.
I choose friends
Who mutually encourage.
I choose to be around people
Who live in integrity.
The choices I make
Proclaim who I am.
They are a statement of
My commitment.
They show how I live.
They show how I love.
The choice is mine.

I release.

No attachment. That is the goal.

Long process.

Learning curve.

Unlearning.

From "I want"

And "I need"

To no wants

And no needs.

From clutter to empty.

From busy to clear.

From needed to free.

From accomplished to unburdened.

I relinquish my commitments.

It is a quiet process.

No one even notices.

Which is the whole point.

Unattachment goes unnoticed.

No attachment is the goal.

Unlearning.

I release.

I seek out people who
Share my perspective.
I am always delighted
To see who comes to the table.
I learn from them.
I study with them.
These friendships are anchored
In what is real.
In magic.
In hiking. In travel.
In meditation.
In reflection.
In respect.
Our meetings may be
Intentional or random.
We call each other in.
We recognize each other.
We connect.
We go our separate ways.
We benefit.
I am always delighted
By those who come to the table.

I feel the energy of the Universe.
I feel the ferocity of Mother Earth.
I notice the emotions of people,
Some in sync with Nature,
Some way out of line.
I feel them all.
We all have that capacity.
My recognition of energy
Does not require me to consume that energy.
I can observe without taking it in.
I can notice without absorbing.
I watch, then I decide.
Do I accept what I see?
Or do I release it?
The choice is mine.
Always.
The choice is mine.
I choose to accept
The energy that
Moves me forward.
The choice is mine.

Unusual weather for this time of year.
This departure from the norm reminds me to
Be aware of changes around me.
My environment transforms,
I have the option to flow with it.
When I resist, my thoughts are foggy.
My body hurts, my equilibrium is disrupted.
But when I flow,
All is well.
My thoughts and actions are
In sync with my soul.
I flow through life,
Aware of changes around me,
In sync with my core.
Unusual weather for this time of year.

How did we get here?

Where are we going?

How do we put aside

A part of what we know?

How do we

Bring into our lives

Something better?

Something higher?

Let the spirit of the season be bright.

Let the spirit of the season be love.

Let the spirit of the season be peace.

Let peace be the message you spread.

Let peace be your reason for being.

Let peace be so quiet and still that

It speaks for itself.

Let peace be so bright that

It lights the world.

Let peace be so strong that

People stand aside

To let it come through.

Let peace be yours.

Let peace be ours.

Let peace be.

ACKNOWLEDGMENTS

There is an old saying: When the student is ready, the teacher appears. My teachers showed up at the right time. When I needed an editor, Reverend Deborah Phillips arrived, with talent in meditation and poetry. When I needed to see my potential, Jim Jordan handed me a mirror. When I needed a publisher who would share my vision, Patricia Marshall showed up with the team of Luminare Press. When I needed guidance on graphics, Matt Pacini was at my door. Thanks to the hundreds of people in TransForMission classes for giving me as much as I gave them. I am grateful for my talented friends at CapRadio (NPR) and Sacramento Public Library. I appreciate the people whose words inspired me to leap, including John Lescroart, Kathleen Sabbagh, Rivkah Sass, Diane Dulberg, Julie Pfitzinger, Jennifer Halm, Nicole Forsyth, Kristi Matal, Lama Yeshe Jinpa, Reverend Richard Burdick, Evan Matsler, Mark Jones, Nick Brunner, the Insight team, Marci Lanza Mitchell, Anne Gambino, Rob Stewart, the Cunninghams, Reverend Dr. Georgia Prescott, Mike Wallace, Leslie Kranz, Kay Ryan, Reverend David Clark, Wayne Manning, Phil Konz and Pam Anderson-Bartholet. I am inspired by the creativity of writers, speakers, musicians, artists and dancers in my community. Thanks to the authors, too many to name, who have visited for interviews. I am fortunate to be in touch with family and classmates around the world, and colleagues from radio and TV stations across the country, who say and write little things that motivate me. Thanks to my long-time work partner, Steve Milne, for his constant, calm presence. Big gratitude for the 100,000 people who listen every week. Without knowing it, they inspired this book and everything I've done for well over 20 years.

53678822R00121